Unsuitable Shoes

Alicia
Stubbersfield

THE COLLECTIVE PRESS

© The Collective Press 1999

Cover design
& Layout

Cataloguing In Publication Data for this book is
available from the British Library

ISBN 1 899449 65 5

Published with the financial support of the
Arts Council of Wales.

Front-cover illustration by Paul Magrs

Main Typeface; Futura Md BT 11pt.

Printed in Great Britain by Redwood Books

For Alan and Joe

"Hope" is the thing with feathers -

That perches in the soul -

Emily Dickinson

Alicia Stubbersfield lives in Wales where she works as a writer, tutor and course leader for creative writing in The Open College of the Arts. Her first collection "The Magician's Assistant" was described in *Poetry Review* as "confidently sensual and subtle...with a tongue-in-cheek approach to landscape."

ACKNOWLEDGEMENTS

I particularly want to thank Gabrielle Ivinson, Paul Magrs and the members of Off the Page for their careful reading of many of these poems. I am grateful to all my friends for their love and support.

Some of these poems have appeared in the following publications:

Iron, Kunapipi, Never Bury Poetry, Outposts, Poetry and Audience, Pretext, Smiths Knoll, Spokes, Staples Competition Edition 1999, The North.

Some poems were prizewinners in the following competitions:

Conwy Arts Festival	1997 and 1998
Ilkley Literature Festival	1996
Lancaster Litfest	1995
The Peterloo Poetry Competition	1996

The poem "Underground" was commissioned by Ledbury Poetry Festival 1998 as part of their "Poets at Work" sessions.

CONTENTS

Slug

I dream snails and their shells,
pellucid swirls of brown,
pale on the inside like sky,
always available, almost weightless.

I would be safe, touching the sides,
seeing light change,
stuck against the comforting
roughness of wall.

I inch my way
towards the secrecy of foliage,
the velvet wrap of earth,
a pebble's dark.

Behind me I leave moon-trail,
lametta glued to stone,
the unanswerable scrawl
of my whole body writing.

Unsuitable Shoes

Sheep are the voices of the damned,
calling out to you as you stumble along,
demanding something you can't give
in this flimsy dress, these crazy shoes.

You're following him along a path
edged with the soft bodies of sheep.
It wasn't what you expected tonight
or what you told yourself was possible.

There is the slightest curve of moon,
the sighing of wind through gorse
still yellow in the half-light, the day's end,
when you are struggling over dried earth.

He slows, takes your hand across the stream,
an owl cries out, searching for voles,
your breath hurts in your chest, a fox slips
away knowing you are too close for comfort.

Red shoes covered in dust, fine leather
holding your feet like ballet pumps
but you're not dancing, only keeping up
while he takes you walking on the mountain.

It was never going to happen again,
you promised yourself after the last time.
This is the last time you said, wrote those
words on the inside of cigarette packets.

You got into the car just the same,
fastened your seat belt quick and tight,
not meaning to go this far, to jump out
lightly, skipping through the wide gate.

How you pretend, how you stay silent
when your feet hurt and the sheep's voices
remind you of where you should be, not here,
not ruining your pretty little shoes.

It Has Come To This

In the box on my desk is a tiny bird skull,
light as paper, pale like today's sky
sullied by this endless November rain.

I know what to do. Tantric sex explains
that ours is a journey of the heart
and we must not touch: I won't start
remembering the terrible smoothness inside
your elbow where the thick blue vein hides,
the cigarette-and-wine taste of you.

I fit this skull over my head, gaze through
the bird's empty eyes, imagine I'm blindfolded.
Close to you I must behave as if I were dead.

Fine bone joins head to needle beak,
too fragile for me to turn away or speak,
so I rehearse fact: the heart is an organ,
purple and streaked, not the valentiney song
we want it to be, beating, beating too fast
so if I touched you it would be like the last
time and each time before that.

In the blue box is a tiny bird skull that
is as light as paper, grey as today's sky
weeping rain, more than even we can cry.

Still Winter

A day to be seduced,
full of false promises
like one starling
mimicking a curlew
but not quite making
that final wild spiral
into air cleared of mist.
Sun edges hills
though our focus stays blurred,
not ready to discard too much
on this day in early January
when wood smoke still ghosts
through villages and I drive
towards you, my mac in the boot.

Skin

I'm changing gear and you cover my hand,
holding us in neutral for a moment.
No-one touched my left hand for years,
I let no-one feel the Braille map of skin
ruched up by thirty-five stitches.

Showing my palm to Madame Petulengro
was an act of faith.
She said it didn't matter,
love lines broken and interrupted,
there'd be two men in my life.

Now I prefer scars to untroubled flesh,
wrinkles spread outwards like tiny wings,
bellies begin to ease.
I put my hand in yours,
you read what's written there.

A Red Map

She remembers throwing the glass,
it shattering against yellow wallpaper,
water dripping, splinters on the floor.
Next the milk bottles, one by one,
smacked on the doorstep.

They took some notice:
wheeled her baby out
so she could rest, checked
she was eating properly,
asked about the doctor's visit.

No-one seemed to see
bits of her were disappearing,
understand how, each day,
another part was missing,
fingers worst of all so she couldn't
fasten a zip or secure a nappy.

Her voice stuck somewhere
far away so she rushed out
of shops without asking.
Now and then laughter bubbled,
spilled out, on and on.

She knew what would help,
looked for it daily in papers,
on television and found it
in car number plates,
the perfect alignment
of tree and lamppost,
three magpies on her lawn.

She lit candles in every room,
checked the doors five times only
before sitting down
with the special knife
she knew was hers,
silver like tonight's moon.

One sliver and then another,
clean and true,
red map-lines slowly forming
to show her the way,
and she'd find it now
she was sure.

Foxgloves

Rain made the whole valley green
and humid like somewhere tropical.
It brought out more foxgloves than ever,
spiking down the hillside near her house.

Poor man's orchids in rich pink
where fairies leave their shoes.
Speckled paths lead into those mouths,
to the guts of an unknown creature.

She picked hundreds of flowers,
flattened them under books or stones,
closed their lips together,
waited for the drying out to happen.

Digitalis contracted her heart,
slowed her pulse right down
until she barely remembered
his skin touching hers.

Her dreams began to be all pink,
the weight of fuschia pressing down,
pale rose on quieter nights
softening outlines, making things hazy.

Hailstones on the window like seeds
rattling in pods close to exploding
while pink spears open cracks through
floorboards, door frames: let themselves in.

Letters Home

Your best handwriting in Quink
using the pen you were given at eleven
for passing that exam to grammar school.
She will compare the shape and style
with your father's, whose character
you have inherited.

Describe the dress you wore,
the jewellery, your hair tied back:
this is the first fiction.
Next you describe his quiet ways,
how he walked you home from a film
along winding pavements,
under yellow street-lights.

Do not mention coffee
or waiting in the kitchen for a kettle,
your back against the fridge,
then green mugs, a bottle of red wine,
how desire tastes in someone else's mouth,
skin warm and slow to give up its salt,
the ease of forgetting.

She can tell her friends about the books,
snack-bars with plastic cups,
lads playing table football
while you read another novel.
Concerts, choirs, the bustle of traffic.
You write his name on the library table,
rub it out, write it again, feel his fingers
reach the softness at the top of your thigh.

Lies like sprinkled glitter,
omissions black as peat bogs
where you hide yourself,
preserve that secret part unseen.

Now you can never tell the truth
or you would prove her right after all.
You will be just like your father
in that other story, told to make you
feel guilty or ashamed or the weight
of years no amount of talking,
or cleaning or hoping can change.

Gin and Sympathy

My mother lights Marlene's Disque Bleu,
admires the tortoiseshell holder,
remembers her own, glossy black, inlaid.

Ash drifts around their chairs, is flicked
away as they talk of the inadequacies
of daughters: each has only one.

Marlene must scrub Maria's lino,
my mother knows, she washes my dishes,
my dusters, sorts out the pairing of socks.

Both women are shocked by our fridges,
our expensive vegetables, lack of red meat,
Marlene explains how to make beef tea.

It is five o'clock somewhere in the world
so my mother opens a gin bottle
which smells like gardenias, like army uniform.

The level in the bottle slips down,
easy as a silk dress bias-cut across
a flat stomach and they begin to remember.

Sticky tape loosens, Marlene's eyes droop,
my mother adjusts her padded bra.
They stretch out good legs.

A low hum begins in Marlene's throat,
"Falling in love again," my mother never
wanted to, is pouring another gin.

Late Afternoon

After the doctor left
and before the undertaker arrived
I cut the old-fashioned roses
I nearly brought you earlier
so you could wake
to their smell in your room.

I stand at the foot of your bed,
no sheet pulled over your head
like they do in films, the duvet
too bulky and wrong somehow,
my hands full of roses, thorns
in my skin, their heads heavy.

I struggle to say impossible things
before I change your bed linen,
hoover , put the flowers
next door in my house and wait
for the men to take you away.

The undertaker sits at my table
chatting about death, babies,
his youngest daughter at Oxford,
how he was a bastard at school
and gave teachers a hard time.

No-one is making me hot, sweet tea
as you are driven off in the hearse,
its windows so clear
anyone could see you.

I sit at my kitchen table
with the undertaker I found in Yellow Pages,
filling in forms on this warm June afternoon,
smiling and nodding,
trying to make decisions,
the air full of the perfume of roses.

Hen

Corn no longer interests her,
she doesn't peck at worms,
gets lost in the others' rush
and barely moves from the gate.

You are sorting through boxes
from my mother's house,
still in our shed after a year,
everything wrapped and hidden.

As you open one after another,
the smell of cigarettes and Arpege
drifts out and I can almost believe
she is standing there beside you.

The red hen is lying down,
her scaly legs to one side,
round eyes blinking in sunshine.
The old cockerel stands nearby.

You show me layers of handbags,
black patent, orange, navy-blue,
crocodile, lizard, beaded for evenings,
one for every outfit over the years.

Another filled with tiny, fancy shoes
with hardly a sign of feet in them.
We close it up, put it away again
for some other time.

Next morning I go out with a bin liner,
but you've moved her already.
I find the flattened bit of dusty earth
and a pale egg.

The Cemetery

Names give them away,
O'Brian, Hennessy, Kavanagh,
lying under stones, exhorting Mary
or some favourite saint
to take care of their immortal souls.

I'm looking for my father.
There are names I recognise,
my art teacher and the district nurse.
Some graves gleam, kept neat
by relatives planting pots of daffodils.
I walk up and down the endless rows,
peering at lettering until my eyes hurt,
slow rain blotches granite.

I find what I'm searching for:
grubby marble, overgrown grass,
the edging stones pushed out by roots.

I kneel here,
pick at thick weeds, dirtying my nails.
I am tucking in bed sheets,
plumping a pillow,
wanting to hold him as I would my child.
In front of me a man busies himself
with trowel, new plants, a bag for rubbish.
He does not look at me
and I don't throw myself down
sobbing or wail out loud.

I just sit, sit on cold stone,
smooth the counterpane again.

A Quiet Man

He waited until the women had gone,
removed his glasses, wound his watch:
two sons at his bedside.
He looked straight at you and died.
It was a good death, we said,
clear, almost uncomplicated, the death
of a careful man who worried
about leaking windowsills, moss on the lawn,
your long hair many years ago.

We read his notebooks, identical, narrow-lined,
filled with details of meals, prices, weather,
forgetting your mother's birthday.
No glimpse of darkness, no hints of a life
other than the insurance manager walking
a deliberate mile every day, learning French
from tapes and folding "The Daily Telegraph"
into a manoeuvrable square.

I still have the half-sucked mint
you gave me in the crematorium
before standing to speak of him,
guessing the man at work,
the Wodehouse reader,
traveller to London or Paris - alone
each September for the last thirty years.

We must go to Montmartre, visit the cafe
where he sat with a thin notebook
watching people pass, writing in biro.
We'll take this small pot of ashes
and scatter them with the wind,
specks of silver carried away
to land, unnoticed, somewhere else.

My Son's Swimming Lesson

You are making this water your own,
learning each careful stroke,
putting your head under, knowing
how to breathe and when not to.
I watch you dive a clean line.

It's ten years since you swam my sea,
that first flick under the skin.
Later you grew vehement,
determined I should recognise you
as you pushed against my dark.

I cannot lower myself into circles
of thin water or blink away the chlorine,
panicking still when out of my depth,
even here despite young lifeguards
patrolling the edge.

Gradually you are gathering yourself up,
co-ordinating muscles, stretching out,
finding confidence in this blue light
where you want me to join you,
to help me look down, carry on breathing.

Llandudno Pier

Sea, the colour of mackerel skins,
heaves against iron pillars
while seagulls fly at face height.
She's holding on to the rail
as if it were an ocean liner
headed out to the horizon, beyond
the Isle of Man, going somewhere.

Light illuminates hotels
like forgotten sweets,
old people going in and out
with umbrellas, pacamacs,
plastic rainhats to keep the perm.
The Great Orme is from the Old Testament,
sunshine through drizzle and Moses
expected, even here among the souvenirs.

In the Seabreeze Cafe, no pierrots
just a thin boy dressed in Everton's colours
serving tea in polystyrene cups
soft on her lips.
Tomorrow it's the hospital
but today she's keeping warm,
listening to rain rattling the windows.

The thin boy wipes down tables,
looks at his watch and it's time to go.
Bunting strains and pulls at ornate posts
like birds anxious to be off.
Notices warn against slipping
as hail stings her skin and she passes
the arcade's gasp of hot air.

There is the hotel they always visited,
every year of her childhood, the same
room, the same food, the chairs still
in rows out on the verandah where her father
sat waiting for them to come back; her hands
full of shiny pebbles to show him, pebbles
dulling even as she carried them home.

Mixed Surgical

Wheels spin like anxiety
circling the ward.
Up and down the corridor,
frustration caught in spokes,
arm muscles growing as legs wither.

Buzzers glow red,
nurses make their way to quiet beds,
or laugh and chat while a faint voice
calls from far away.
Swing doors bang, the clock snaps.

No-one stops him as he hurtles
back and back countless times.
The sister argues with the registrar,
"I've got a lady vomiting."
leaves him standing, suddenly young.

She lies in the half-light,
bits of tissue stuffed in her ears,
a trolley rattling,
blood and lymph slowly draining
away into the plastic bottle.

Tomorrow there's a wedding,
some kind of hope in the day room
before it's too late.
The bridegroom takes his morphine
while those wheels turn and turn all night.

Tumour: the hypotheses

Sometimes she thought she'd made it herself,
unshed tears distilled or loss made stone.
Was that it?
Her cat's eye marble
purple at its centre, waiting to spill
when they sliced it for the microscope.

"Only doormats get breast cancer."
Her skin bristled with coir,
keeping things clean, mopping up
and straightening the edges.

Too much mothering was easy to prove,
feeding her son on demand,
that small mouth clamped and sucking,
his cry waking her two, three times
each night, but what peace it gave,
street lights holding everything back.

Could it be just random?
Or an act of God to bring her up short,
take notice, eat her greens, and go for walks.
The pale line where a breast used to be
maps new directions,
disappearing into her own skin.

Chemo

They dress up for chemotherapy,
fancy hats, wigs straightened,
the last shadow of eyebrow
painted in.

They smile through lipstick,
bright as hospital lights,
read magazines, comfort
their husbands who don't know
what to say.

Menopause brought on with drugs,
hot flushes not PMS
and dreams of children,
breasts imitated by new technology,
pale-pink and feeling
like cold skin.

You can tell them by their gloves
worn to keep hands hot enough
to raise a geography of thick veins
whose knots will open
to let the needle in.

That slow, gentle needle
so there's no bruise,
only a tiny speck of blood
to mark the place.
The nurses take a pride in it.

On the way home they're waiting
for the nausea, the weakness,
the way they will wait the rest
of their lives for a sign,
a tiny lump, or indigestion, blood
in the wrong place at the wrong time.

Crows on the Lawn

Five crows on the lawn
celebrating their black mass.
It has become night where they are,
the darkness death will bring
or depression's beak pecking at glass.

She has lost track of herself,
short-haired in the mirror,
fatter: fingers too big for her ring,
thighs sturdy, skin pulled tight.
She's still in there somewhere,
peering out and wondering.

One crow now in the apple tree,
a huge black question mark
above the ball of mistletoe.
Perhaps each cancels out the other.
In India, crows mean good fortune
but not here, not here.

A HUNDRED YEARS OF DREAMS

1. She Falls Asleep

Beauty dreams the twentieth century
pricked into sleep at the year's hinge
as a faraway clock spills each second
until midnight and the spindle falls.

Her father carries her to the bed we imagine,
covers her with heaven's cloths, the dim
of twilight embroidered with stars. Fair hair
clouds pillows, breath whispers into the room.

A long film unspools on her mind's screen,
monochrome at first, women in long skirts.
The bed is hard; she is held down by straps,
by a tube wrenching open her gagging throat.

Hand-painted banners make samplers
of streets outside prisons, outside Parliament.
Beauty's wrists bleed as chains tighten.
The racehorse's hooves kick blackness into her skull.

She hears guns howl, boots stamping down mud,
sea slapping against grizzled cliffs.
Cards arrive signed in pale ink, "always yours."
Her hands flutter with white feathers.

Men fly but she is Amelia dressed in leather,
steadying those outstretched wings,
below are heaving waves, a puzzle of land,
above just empty spaces pierced with light.

2. She Receives the First Prince

This prince sees no hedge to bar his way,
needs no sword to hack aside blackthorn,
spike-headed thistle, the bindweed's tendrils
as he arrives at your door.

You have expected him Beauty,
will allow him to wait in the hall.
You have seen him many times already,
about to carry you into his tent's dark
mouth where desert sand swirls like confetti,
or ready to whisk you across a dance floor,
holding you close enough to touch your skin.

He wants a bride sugared in taffeta
who will understand his need
to ride, shoot, stay late at the office.
You will take his coat, pour him a whisky.

His khaki is splattered with someone else's blood,
he comes home from the war, is a leader of men.
You watch miners disappear into earth's darkness
while soot hardly sullies his white linen jacket.

The prince feels your breath's slight agitation,
outside castle windows swifts scythe the air,
you are mapping stars, the sun's bright angles,
don't notice the fumble of his lips.

3. She's Never Had It So Good

Beauty stands in her kitchen,
ration books lost in formica drawers,
pineapple sweetening Sunday lunch
and the New Look swirling about her ankles.

Red and yellow lino covers black and white
for ever as rock and roll crackles petticoats
and she learns to backflip for Buddy Holly,
getting home by ten o' clock.

Soon she is a doll, false eyelashes blink
into a psychedelic future while she dances
in plastic boots, face and lips Quant-pale,
boys rev scooters, girls on the back laugh.

Beauty's room is San Francisco,
Janis sings and incense burns,
she scatters flowers, is moving on,
smelling freedom's resin not far away.

4. She Receives the Second Prince

Look into a mirror, Beauty,
your prince reflects you.
Breathe on her,
feel her soft lips
reaching to touch yours.

She will know you,
each sweet crevice,
dark places hidden
from everyone.
Rise up, stretch your arms,
sink into the warmth of her.

You can go together
into the room
men cannot enter,
cannot even imagine,
though they try.

She is a pool rippling
at the forest heart.
You will dream language,
travel to the core of light,
flying without a net.

Wear this scarlet cloak, Beauty,
wolves will howl
but they can't reach the moon
which is all yours

if you open your eyes,
turn silver over
in your heart
and take her now.

5. She Thinks She Can Do It All

Where is Beauty now?
As the fleet sails out to some small island
and the new Boudicca rides her chariot
on a forsaken beach to a chorus of weeping.
There is no horizon, no difference
between land and the drained sky.

We might find her weaving wool
through a wire fence as tears
drip green into her eyes.

From the other side,
men see tessellations,
jigsaws of thirty thousand women.
Beauty learns to go limp
in the policeman's arms.

Or does she think the wars are won?
Leaving the baby smell at home,
her shoulders wide, her skirt narrow,
stroking the fine, shiny plastic
of her machines.

Watch her skin slacken just the same,
despite creams, the therapist's touch
on her aching head.

Round her neck a crystal flashes change,
she decides what is possible.
Far away behind thorns,
she hears the sound
of the century's clock grinding.

6. She's On Her Own

It begins in your spine
as though slow fingers are touching
each separate vertebra, stroking bone
through fine skin, still pliant and stretched.
A faint fluttering at your temples,
the slightest tightening across your forehead.
Fingers flex around some imagined thing,
your horse's reins, the smooth curves of a spindle.

You have seen them Beauty, lined up,
carrying gifts to win you,
craving that first soft awakening
when your mouth changes
and you taste desire
so nothing is ever the same again.
Now you know them all,
their teasing voices, pressing lips,
hands that would busy about you,
unbuttoning, demanding too much.

Nothing has changed and everything
through this playing of it all,
watching a long spool unwind:
you are made of stars.
Your eyelids flinch,
there is a clenching and unclenching,
crowds watching a ferris wheel cranking,
beginning to turn as bells spin
a golden line from steeple to steeple
across the land.

Images slip away, melt into water
running down mountains,
or roll into messages carried by pigeons,
dark affirmations against the sky.
In graveyards stone angels
widen their wings, ready to fly.
Cows in every shippon begin lowing,
curlews bubble silver spirals
and sheep gaze beyond valleys
in a wild surmise.

Now Beauty, now you are waking
as the year's hinge opens
and lets you through
with no father, or mother, or prince
to carry you, surround you with roses.
The hedge has gone,
leaving only the scent of lilac.
January sun is weak
but promises warmth on stone walls
and the determined push of green.
There is silence and pale yellow light
as you sit up, plait your long hair,
begin again.

The Heart of Robert the Bruce

(taken into battle by his lieutenant)

Not a bleeding heart anymore
but plucked from behind his ribs
and brought here in a secret box.

How do you keep a heart?
Salt it, cure it, harden it
until the soft beat disappears.

Take it out, place it in your hand,
feel the unbearable weight of it,
the shape fitting your palm.

Test the parabola so you can throw
a perfect arc and it will land far off.
You will find it, you will always find it.

His heart next to yours at night,
a cream silk handkerchief wrapped
around this lump of darkening flesh.

The purple soon fades, the scarlet
of hibiscus opening silent mouths
beside your tent is soon gone.

He asked you to do it. Now you can't
get away from some imagined tattoo
sounding you into the thick of it.

He's urging you on into this hot battle,
your two hearts hammering and his voice
telling you, again, there's nothing to lose.

Betrayal

from "Crowning with Thorns" by Hironymous Bosch

Brought here by hope, by sweet words,
Even the crown's seduction as each
Thorn draws you towards Him:
Red specks bubble and fall. Judas turns
Away while Peter hears the faintest crowing.
You are only flesh
And a cotton shift dropping in folds.
Love them: there is no alternative.

Gift

I want to buy you glass
fine, clear, green as hawthorn
or the far away blue of April.

Crystal glitters all around me,
lit up for Christmas, tied with
ribbons, resting in fake snow.

I choose this plain tumbler
remembering whisky we drank straight
from your bottle on a bleak hilltop,

strands of hair touching my face,
a hare bucking past us
silvered by March sun.

The young man wraps your present
in layers of tissue for me to carry
like a chalice through city crowds.

Venus Speaks

from "Venus and Mars" by Sandro Botticelli

I have become expert
in the telling of lies,
at slipping away unnoticed,
changing before he sees
grass stains rising on my gown.

You just lie there, head back,
tiny gasps of breath warming
the air, ignoring the satyrs
wearing your helmet,
blowing a conch, poking fun.

I wait and watch your chest
rise, fall, rise again.
I rehearse my story, can describe
the anxiety of wasps, a woodpecker
thrumming, my friend's conversation.

Not this. Not your hair streaked
darker red with sweat,
the coldness of your armour
plucking my chiffon,
the haste of your unbuckling.

Quickly I can undress and dress again,
fastening the brooch you gave me
without fumbling.
I have picked myrtle for you
to take away from here.

You can crush it between your fingers,
let the scent rise
until you smell this grove and us here.
I tuck one dark sprig into my plait
saving it for later.

Contingency

I have waited here before
in rain stirring the Thames
to darkness, filling my silly shoes
and curling my hair wildly.
You were stopped by the weather,
stuck somewhere on the other side.

We tried again in winter,
ice froze roads and railways
or we could have danced on the river,
lit bonfires and roasted oxen.
I sifted flour over cherries, beat sugar
and butter, licked the bowl clean.

In summer everything was hazy,
sun turned water into a mirror
where I saw my face practising a smile.
Neon decorated buildings like cakes
and strings of diamante lights hung
in air too calm for its own good.

We keep on trying, letters come and go.
Your voice on my answer machine
surprises me into planning another day.
I listen to weather reports and hope
for a mild spring, not too many tulips,
flat blue sky and my hair left unwashed.

Disappointment is just another train
clacking over Hungerford Bridge,
chocolate powder dusting my mouth
and the saxophone's notes circling
while I sit still, interrupted suddenly
by quick footsteps passing.

All I Can Do

I was all creature,
part of the waves pulling me in,
somersaulting beyond the cliff edge
to where sand falls away
and no-one can touch bottom.

Sea and sky are one there,
stars pierce black water,
moon breaks on the surface.
My body span through tiny fish
kissing my skin, nibbling all of me.

He spat me out, left me
gritty, drying on rocks.
He went on the night train,
the station smelt of piss, stale burgers,
I counted each carriage as it passed.

I paint my nails red,
shape them into shells
soothed by the emery board.
Sometimes I drink vodka or coffee
until my heart races and I walk home.

Rain shines on pavements,
late shoppers dart into doorways.
My umbrella stays furled
as I walk down to the sea,
watching light shiver in deep water.

Underground

Hold on, count backwards
from a hundred and wave
as he disappears into the crowd.
Stare at the map, note each station,
do not look at the woman reading
The Independent and crying.

You give yourself up to the rattle,
the curved roof and the lurching
carriage tight with other people,
trying not to recall his hand
touching yours before he left,
but smelling him anyway,
here among the Calvin Klein,
hot bodies and sharpness of sweat.

Outside is dark,
the recklessness of tracks.
Concentrate on artificial light
holding everything back.
Above you he walks those streets,
sees you twenty times a day
but it isn't you, will never be you.

Sometimes, in that space
just before sleep, you know there is
a connection like water underground
deep and peaty and hidden
until the rain comes,
when it spills out from black earth,
sudden and frightening.

The Reunion

Thirteen circle our table
but there's nothing left to betray
as I swizzle my chopsticks and you spear
a prawn from the dish gliding round.
We're counting out husbands, wives, children,
describing jobs, houses, success, not quite
colouring in the spaces from lives flickering past.

In Piccadilly Gardens the ferris wheel spins
empty seats, still too early for girls screaming
into the sky though sirens pierce Manchester
as we walk uneven pavements to the Conti.
The Greeks on the door seem to know us
twenty years on and now women pay to drink
sweet wine, push by hot bodies tilted together.

Old tunes play on the juke box,
you take me down to dance,
our shoes sticky on this beery floor.
Years begin to trickle away like sweat
and I taste youth's salt on my tongue.
Here we can tell the truth, you and me,
your hands around my waist just like last time.

They were old enough to know better

than to sit in a shadowy corner
sipping fizzy drinks through ice
and talking, just talking for ages
discovering it all again,
the way he jutted his chin
how she looked sad sometimes

his long fingers tasting spiced food
in bright colours, his pale green chilli
her salad softened with yoghurt
warm bread soaking up sauce
and the coffee in Aladdin's silver lamp
sweet, hot, scented with cardamom

before they sneaked away
holding hands, undoing buttons
crumpling wool and crepe
finding desire again almost unexpectedly
like October sun skewing through trees
reddening the leaves before winter.

Shoot Out

It was years later he told her
about that first night in Blackpool,
lights making the whole town
into a drag queen's dress,

how, after a few beers, egged on
by wild music filling the fairground,
he and his friend fired guns
at rows of tin ducks to win her.

At first she laughed, imagining
a rifle tucked into his shoulder,
the care he'd take to line it up,
fingers gentle on the trigger,

suddenly squeezing, one duck
after another, falling backwards
before he turned to her
and gave her the fluffy teddy.

One night she dreamed of his friend
strolling down her street, hands ready
at his hips, black hat low on his brow.
A noon sun bleached tarmac to dust.

She surprised herself as he lifted her
on to the warmth of his horse's back,
and they cantered into the distance
towards a thin pencil line of smoke.

Human Cannonball

I am the closed hinge of myself
wedged in here, waiting for the word.
Outside there is the thickness of heat,
the stench of animals and almost silence.

I hear tigers roar in the distance,
metal muffles everything until it stops
making sense and the only truth is here.
Cold touching my skin, seeping into me.

I have to stay small, I have to fit
inside this tube which goes on forever.
A circle of yellow above me,
my knees against my chest, fingers curled.

My father parades the ring,
leads the cannon so it is placed just so.
There is a net and I will land like a fish
scooped from water to be thrown back.

My flesh stays tight over bones
that flex and bend and give in
to his demands, his watching
when I eat: I mustn't grow too big.

Beyond this iron casing there is air,
animals loping backwards and forwards,
pegs hammered into rough grass,
holding it all down.

He controls time and the force needed
to send me into that tremendous arc.
I stretch out for a moment, flying, flying,
before the net clutches me: saved again.

A Night Out

I'm almost used to street lights.
I prefer the comfort of dark
but those golden pools falling
on some young girl's shoulders,
on the little blue pulse at the side
of a long neck, excite me.

Safety is the scent of damp wood,
my palms flat against the edges,
earth's gentle shifting as moles
and worms tunnel and squirm.
I know it will come,
that slow tingle through my body,
the itch of desire turning my head.

Then I'm strong, can push up the lid,
scramble out, stretch my spine
and walk, unsteady at first, away
from the graveyard, down into town.
I am dressed in my Ossie Clark,
black crepe swirls above my ankles,
a little mildewed but smart enough.

I have until dawn to take her,
to walk along the canal path.
She will trust me when I slip
my arm around her,
my hand in the small of her back.

I taste blood before it's in my mouth,
before its thick weight on my tongue
as if it's melting but staying warm,
body-heat as it slides into my throat,
the sweet metal of it filling me:
her faraway moan.

THE RIVALS

i. Cheltenham

The north is falling away from me,
I practise "grass, grass, grass"
among strangers whose cool accents
echo across curved balconies.

You hurry towards me, holding anemones,
their colours gaudy in unexpected heat.
Leaves turn brown, maggots burst
into iridescent wings and my skin burns.

You take me to an antique shop
where the smell of mothballs and old
perfume drops like gauze over furs,
ball gowns, peach-coloured slippery satin.
We try on hats, smile madly in the mirror.

The dress you choose is pale-blue,
black stripes swirl across my body.
In this shop, in this dress,
I am Marlene Dietrich.

In my room, I wear the dress,
lie with my arm behind my head,
watching you mix paints.
Later you undo fifty hooks and eyes,
trace the hard bumps of my spine.

We are in a glass half-full of wine,
sun is gilding the tall window,
glitters for a moment in my hair
before darkness licks away its blaze.

ii. The Party

Behind us the party is dissolving
"Say something northern."
Richard's voice is newly American,
revving a Harley along wide roads.

I stumble outside where the garden
is a carousel speeding up until vomit
splashes my shoes, drips from roses
almost luminous in the pale evening.

Richard dresses windows, arranges women,
changes their clothes, abandons them
in corners, leaves torsos naked on the street.
He sits with you, so close your heads touch.

Silence blots up your thoughts, his skin
is still tanned, firm across strong bones
not like my freckled arms.
You arrange to meet again.

Talk circles from a stone dropped
into the past's dark pool, "Will it make
any difference?" Your mouth on his,
the roughness of his chin rubbing yours.

I am somewhere else.

Blue flames flinch in the gas-fire,
steady, flinch again as two men touch
for the first time, knock over a wine bottle
their breath quickening into faint cries.

iii. Cheltenham

Exhaust fumes sour the air,
catching your throat, Richard's
taste still bruising your tongue.
You kick a can across concrete.

Dusty windows reflect your face,
behind you I am wearing your clothes,
velvet jeans and white shirt.
My cheekbones ready to slice you.

I dream of you dancing with Richard
in a ballroom under a glittering bauble
which twirls light into shivering pieces.
I sit in the corner, just watching.

You lean towards me, not smiling
but reaching out and fear opens
my ribs, grabs my heart, shakes it.

iv. London

London is stinking in August heat,
piles of rubbish rot down back streets,
taxis spit out grey fumes
choking back my first breath there.

I follow you and Richard on to the tube,
talk myself through claustrophobia
as doors squelch shut and we rattle along
to Liberty's and Art Nouveau glass.

I choose shops instead of the Tate,
leave you together to exclaim
over technique, to rush loudly
from room to room.

Mick Jagger leers on every street,
his shorts half-zipped, tempting
women to get their fingers sticky.
Tracks from the record tangle my head.

On Paddington Station two men kiss,
mouth on mouth, as you and Richard
giggle up, grab me and run to the train.
I sit opposite you both, silent and waiting

v. Cheltenham

Other palms had shuffled these cards
left clammy questions on the outside.
Sarina turns over card after card
laying out your life on a plastic cloth.

My face blurs Richard's,
his mouth demands an answer.
A fat red heart pierced with swords,
clouds bursting their dark skins.

You stare at the Fool ready to step
over the mountain's edge, ahead
the Ace of Swords sharp and silver
in a knight's hand and you know.

You have to tell me, speak those words
I shall barely understand,
my skin shrivels until I'm too small,
the sword is rising in your head.

vi. The River

Saturday shoppers swallow you
and I get the bus to Sapperton,
feeling sick as it sways, jerks
over bumps, tourists squealing.

Blowsy poppies smear grass,
midges agitate in clear sky,
water pours over limestone,
a herringbone of light.

The rhythm rubs away
last night's conversation.
My fingers stroking your forehead,
telling you it would be all right.

Tiny bites redden and itch
I see your face disappearing,
you are lying on Richard's bed,
Shadows wince against the wall.

He unbuttons your jeans
slips heavy cotton over bone,
your cock released into his mouth,
your hands in his hair.

I know how it feels to stroke you
with my tongue, to hear you call
my name, over and over....

vii. Cheltenham

You leave the note under a bowl of anemones,
gaze at their black centres, remember my eyes
backlit by evening sun and desire for you.

Downstairs Richard waits for you to run out,
fasten your helmet and push your hands deep
into the pockets of his leather jacket: ride away.

I expect silence as I open the door,
a certain emptiness where your records were,
half-empty shelves and pale patches on the walls.

I read your spiky blue writing, slowly pick out
flower after flower, scattering petals over the bed,
lift up the heavy bowl, dribbling water and bits of green.

The window is open so I throw the bowl.
It bursts on the concrete: a glass balloon
exploding thousands of bright fragments.

viii. The Room

Separation blows dust into my skull.
I am all bone.
Shadows paint lilac under my eyes,
I speak words that stick,
cough out dry tears.
My hands are fists tight by my side,
I sleep in your white shirt,
wake smelling of you.

It would be easy to wrap black swathes
around my body,
a jet necklace binding my throat.
You are not dead.

You are wearing a big coat, selling furniture,
living with Richard, the man who dresses windows.
His smooth-skinned mannequins stand stiff-legged,
their eyes, their vaginas, dry and bloodless.
Your spine arches under his touch.

Night after night, I stand by my window
while lightning wrenches open the sky.
I go back to my empty bed,
wait for some kind of rain-drenched dawn.

ix. Cheltenham

When I dared visit you I took flowers,
iris with yellow tongues ready to slip out.
I was afraid though you made soup
and kept your distance, the one between
words already stretched and unravelling.

I wanted you to wind me back,
gather me up like washing
before the rain comes.
Now I dream of those flowers opening
in your room, exposing their creamy throats.

My love for you is a strawberry mark
slapped across my face, hardly hidden
by the make-up I smear over it.
I hear friends snigger, discussing size, shape,
how it mars an otherwise desirable body.

Since you left I am aware of maroon dye
seeping inwards, clogging up my lymph glands,
forming marbles in sticky places.
I roll them along under my skin until
they make a hard little halo around my heart.

x. Years Later

You know where you're going
as you pass the playground
where mothers remember
feeling dizzy on swings.
Stop for a moment at the lake
watching one swan ripple along.

Oxfam shoes let in the damp,
take a swig of vodka,
walk over a little bridge,
staying with the path, winding its way.
You sat on that bench having your photo taken
twenty years ago when you pouted like Dietrich.

Here are rhododendron bushes,
flowers almost out, purple and pink
pressing against darkness,
hiding the brick walls of the gents' toilet.
A man is waiting, you don't know who he is
but it doesn't matter as you walk towards him.

The local papers will name only you,
will not mention his tongue in your mouth,
sweat cooling on hot skin so you feel
young again like the photographs you saved.
They will not explain fear or excitement, or the way
a heart beats, whether you want it to or not.

Latest Publications

Private People.   *Edited by John Jones*
'self portraits in verse'   ISBN 1 899449 50 7
£5.95

Singing to Seals.   *David A. Hill*
ISBN 1 899449 55 8
£5.95

Making It.   *Ric Hool*
ISBN 1 899449 45 0
£5.95

More titles available on request

How You Can Help

You can support The Collective by ordering any of the above from your local bookshop or direct from the address on the facing page. The money raised goes back into publishing poetry, supporting poets both new and established. You can further support poetry through subscription to poetry magazines and by attending poetry readings at venues throughout the UK. Look out for Collective run events or, if you would like one in your area, get in touch with the Co-ordinator, address as before.

About # The Collective

e-mail   john.jones6@which.net

The Collective is a non-profit-making organisation formed in 1990 to promote and publish contemporary poetry.   Funds are raised through a series of poetry events held in and around South Wales, mainly the Abergavenny area. Many major poets have read for the organisation and been strongly supported by *'new writers'* from Wales and farther afield. The backing and generosity of fellow writers is a cornerstone of The Collective's success.   Vital funding comes from public bodies including the Arts Council of Wales and donations are often received in support of the movement from members of the public. If you would like to find out more about The Collective and its work then contact:

The Co-ordinator
The Collective
Penlanlas Farm
Llantilio Pertholey
Y-Fenni
Gwent
NP7 7HN
Cymru
U.K.

fish